St. Patrick's Day Exp

Size: **Locomotive:** 8¼ inches W x 4⅝ inches H x 3¾ inches D (21cm x 11.8cm x 9.5cm)
Car: 4⅞ inches W x 2⅞ inches H x 3¾ inches D (12.4cm x 7.3cm x 9.5cm)

Skill Level: Beginner

Materials

- ❏ 3 sheets clear 7-count plastic canvas
- ❏ 13 (3-inch) plastic canvas radial circles
- ❏ Medium weight yarn as listed in color key
- ❏ Uniek Needloft metallic craft cord as listed in color key
- ❏ 1½ inches (3.8cm) chain
- ❏ 2 (2-inch/5.1cm) pieces white stem wire
- ❏ #16 tapestry needle
- ❏ Hot-glue gun

Stitching Step by Step

Locomotive

1 Cut engine sides piece, engine front, cab sides A and B, cab front and back, cab roof, two smokestack sides, smokestack front/back piece and engine/cab base from 7-count plastic canvas according to graphs. Also cut two strips 1 hole x 20 holes for large wheel rods; two strips 1 hole x 12 holes for small wheel rods; and one strip holes x 25 holes for headlamp sides.

2 Cut one headlamp, four small wheels and four large wheels from plastic canvas circles according to graphs, cutting away gray areas.

3 Stitch engine sides and front; cab sides, front, back and roof; smokestack sides and front/back; headlamp and wheels according to graphs. Base will remain unstitched.

4 Using white/gold metallic craft cord throughout, work Continental Stitches down center of headlamp sides strip; Overcast one long edge. Overcast all wheels and wheel rods.

5 *Engine:* Gently bend engine sides around engine front, matching red dots. Using craft cord and green yarn according to graphs, Whipstitch engine front to engine sides.

6 *Cab:* Using light green yarn, Whipstitch cab front, sides and back together along side edges, making sure engineers face toward front of locomotive.

7 Using green yarn, Whipstitch roof to assembled cab; Whipstitch curved back edge of engine sides to cutout edge of cab front. Using light green yarn and craft cord according to graphs, Whipstitch assembled cab/engine to unstitched base.

8 *Smokestack:* Gently bend smokestack front/back piece around edge of one smokestack side piece, matching red dots at bottom of smokestack. Using green yarn throughout, Whipstitch side to front/back piece. Whipstitch remaining side piece to unfinished edge; Overcast bottom edges.

9 *Headlamp:* Gently bend headlamp sides strip into a ring. Using craft cord throughout, Whipstitch ring to edge of headlamp, Whipstitching ends of ring together. Overcast unfinished edge.

10 *Assembly:* Referring to photo throughout, hot-glue headlamp to engine front; hot-glue smokestack to engine. Hot-glue two large wheels and large wheel rod to each side of cab with bottom edges even. Hot-glue two small wheels and small wheel rod to each side of engine with bottom edges even.

Car

1 Cut four car sides and four car ends from 7-count plastic canvas according to graphs. Also cut two strips 1 hole x 12 holes for small wheel rods; and one piece 28 holes x 20 holes for car base.

2 Cut four small wheels from plastic canvas circle according to graph, cutting away gray areas.

3 Stitch two car sides, two car ends and all wheel according to graphs. Remaining car sides, ends an base will remain unstitched.

4 Using white/gold metallic craft cord throughou Overcast wheels and wheel rods.

5 Holding an unstitched piece against the reverse sid of a matching car side or end, Whipstitch car side and ends together along corners using craft cord and gree yarn according to graphs, and working through all layers.

6 Using green yarn, Whipstitch assembled car t base, working through all layers. Using craft cor Whipstitch top edges.

7 *Assembly:* Referring to photo throughout, hot-glu two wheels and wheel rod to each side of car wi bottom edges even. Using stem wire, attach ends of cha to car and locomotive.

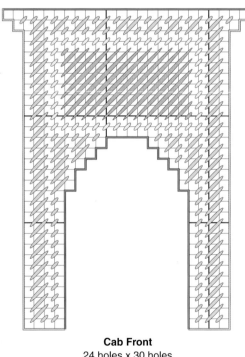

Cab Front
24 holes x 30 holes
Cut 1

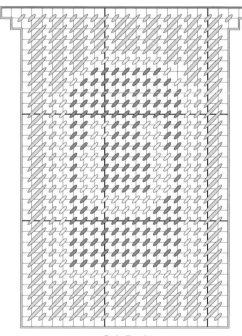

Cab Back
24 holes x 30 holes
Cut 1

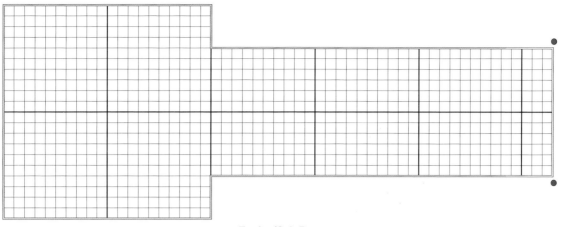

Engine/Cab Base
53 holes x 20 holes
Cut 1, do not stitch

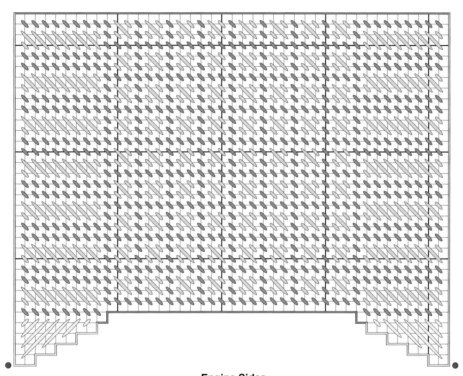

Engine Sides
42 holes x 33 holes
Cut 1

COLOR KEY

Yards	Medium Weight Yarn	
39 (35.7m)		Green
28 (25.7m)		Light green
4 (3.7m)		White
3 (2.8m)		Light gray
1 (1m)		Brown
1 (1m)		Peach
1 (1m)		Red
1 (1m)		Rust
Metallic Craft Cord		
23 (21.1m)		White/gold #55007

Color number given is for Uniek Needloft metallic craft cord.

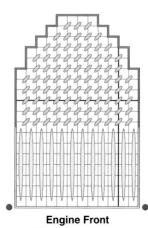

Engine Front
12 holes x 18 holes
Cut 1

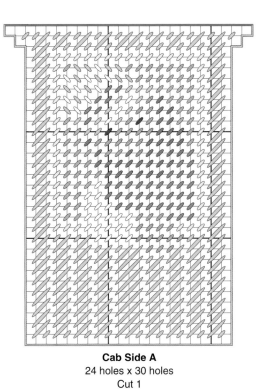

Cab Side A
24 holes x 30 holes
Cut 1

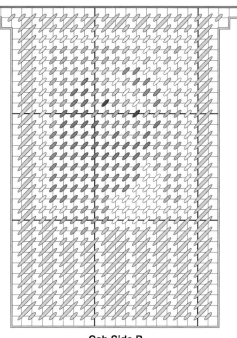

Cab Side B
24 holes x 30 holes
Cut 1

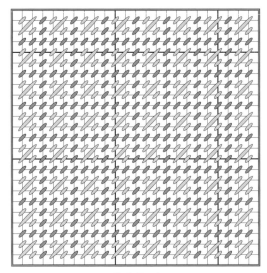

Cab Roof
24 holes x 24 holes
Cut 1

COLOR KEY		
Yards	**Medium Weight Yarn**	
39 (35.7m)		Green
28 (25.7m)		Light green
4 (3.7m)		White
3 (2.8m)		Light gray
1 (1m)		Brown
1 (1m)		Peach
1 (1m)		Red
1 (1m)		Rust
	Metallic Craft Cord	
23 (21.1m)		White/gold #55007

Color number given is for Uniek Needloft metallic craft cord.

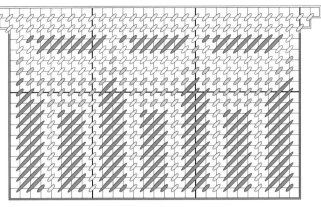

Car Side
32 holes x 18 holes
Cut 4, stitch 2

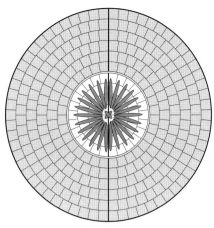

Large Wheel
Cut 4 from 3-inch
radial circles,
cutting away gray areas

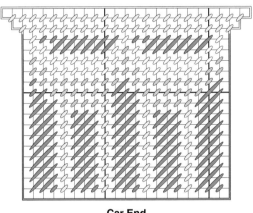

Car End
24 holes x 18 holes
Cut 4, stitch 2

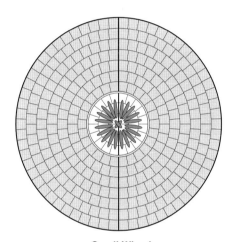

Small Wheel
Cut 8 from 3-inch
radial circles,
cutting away gray areas

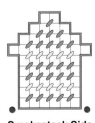

Smokestack Side
8 holes x 9 holes
Cut 2

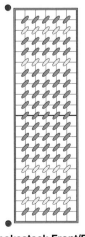

Smokestack Front/Back
6 holes x 20 holes
Cut 1

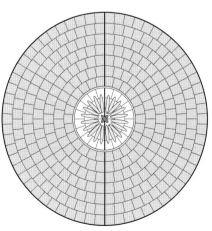

Headlamp
Cut 1 from 3-inch
radial circle,
cutting away gray areas

Easter Express

Size: **Locomotive:** 8 inches W x 6¼ inches H x
3½ inches D (20.3cm x 15.9cm x 8.9cm)
Car: 4½ inches W x 4 inches H x 4½ inches D
(11.4cm x 10.2cm x 11.4cm)

Skill Level: Beginner

Materials

❑ 3 sheets clear 7-count plastic canvas
❑ 13 (3-inch) plastic canvas radial circles
❑ Medium weight yarn as listed in color key
❑ 1½ inches (3.8cm) chain
❑ 2 (2-inch/5.1cm) pieces white stem wire
❑ #16 tapestry needle
❑ Hot-glue gun

Stitching Step by Step

Locomotive

1 Cut engine sides piece, engine front, cab sides A and B, cab front and back, two cab roofs, two smokestack sides, smokestack front/back piece and engine/cab base from 7-count plastic canvas according to graphs. Also cut four strips 1 hole x 12 holes for wheel rods; and one strip 2 holes x 25 holes for headlamp sides.

2 Cut one headlamp, four small wheels and four larg[e] wheels from plastic canvas circles according [to] graphs, cutting away gray areas.

3 Stitch engine sides and front; cab sides, fron[t,] back and roofs; smokestack sides and front/back[,] headlamp and wheels according to graphs. Base w[ill] remain unstitched.

4 When background stitching is complete, Backstitc[h] bunny's mouth on cab sides and back using 2 pl[ies] separated from a length of black yarn.

5 Using pink yarn, work Continental Stitches dow[n] center of headlamp sides strip; Overcast one lon[g] edge. Using yellow yarn, Overcast all wheel rods. Usin[g] light green yarn, Overcast all wheels.

6 *Engine:* Gently bend engine sides around engin[e] front, matching red dots. Using lavender and pin[k] yarn, Whipstitch engine front to engine sides accordin[g] to graphs.

7 *Cab:* Using pink, lavender and yellow yarn accordin[g] to graphs, Whipstitch cab front, sides and bac[k] together along side edges, making sure bunny enginee[r] face toward front of locomotive. Using pink yarn, Overca[st] top edges. Using lavender yarn, Whipstitch curved bac[k] edge of engine sides to cutout edge of cab front.

8 Using yellow, lavender and light green yarn according to graphs, Whipstitch assembled cab/engine to unstitched base.

9 *Roof:* Using green yarn throughout, Whipstitch roof pieces together along one long edge; Overcast remaining edges. Hot-glue roof to cab.

10 *Smokestack:* Gently bend smokestack front/back piece around edge of one smokestack side piece, matching red dots at bottom of smokestack. Using pink yarn throughout, Whipstitch side to front/back piece. Whipstitch remaining side piece to unfinished edge; Overcast bottom edges.

11 *Headlamp:* Gently bend headlamp sides strip into a ring. Using pink yarn throughout, Whipstitch ring to edge of headlamp, Whipstitching ends of ring together. Overcast unfinished edge.

12 *Assembly:* Referring to photo throughout, hot-glue headlamp to engine front; hot-glue smokestack to engine. Hot-glue two large wheels and wheel rod to each side of cab with bottom edges even. Hot-glue two small wheels and wheel rod to each side of engine with bottom edges even.

Car

1 Cut eight car sides, two car base top/bottom pieces, two car base sides and two car base ends from 7-count plastic canvas according to graphs. Also cut two strips 1 hole x 12 holes for wheel rods.

2 Cut four small wheels from plastic canvas circles according to graph, cutting away gray areas.

3 Stitch four car sides, one car base top/bottom piece, both car base sides, both car base ends and all wheels according to graphs. Remaining car sides and second base top/bottom piece will remain unstitched.

4 Using yellow yarn, Overcast wheel rods. Using light green yarn, Overcast wheels.

5 Holding an unstitched piece against the reverse side of a matching car side, and using pink and lavender yarn according to graphs, Whipstitch car sides together along corners, working through all layers.

6 Using pink yarn throughout, Whipstitch bottom edges of assembled car sides to stitched base top, around edges of unstitched area in center. Whipstitch top edges of car.

7 *Base:* Using green yarn throughout, Whipstitch ends of car base side and end strips together to form shallow rectangle. Whipstitch assembled sides and ends to unstitched car base bottom. Whipstitch remaining edges to car base top.

8 *Assembly:* Referring to photo throughout, hot-glue two wheels and wheel rod to each side of car with bottom edges even. Using stem wire, attach ends of chain to car and locomotive.

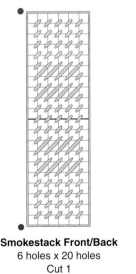

Smokestack Front/Back
6 holes x 20 holes
Cut 1

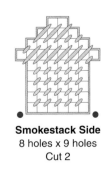

Smokestack Side
8 holes x 9 holes
Cut 2

COLOR KEY	
Yards	**Medium Weight Yarn**
32 (29.3m)	■ Lavender
29 (26.6m)	□ Pink
17 (15.6m)	■ Green
15 (13.8m)	□ Yellow
14 (12.9m)	■ Light green
6 (5.5m)	□ White
5 (4.6m)	■ Rose
4 (3.7m)	□ Light blue
4 (3.7m)	■ Gray
1 (1m)	■ Black
1 (1m)	■ Blue
1 (1m)	■ Dark gold
1 (1m)	■ Gold
╱ Black (2-ply) Backstitch	

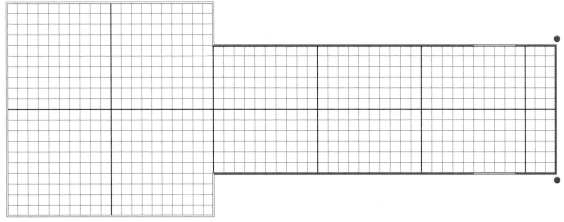

Engine/Cab Base
53 holes x 20 holes
Cut 1, do not stitch

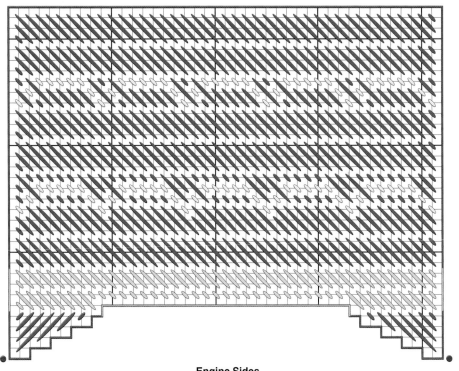

Engine Sides
42 holes x 33 holes
Cut 1

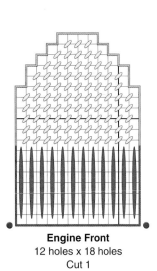

Engine Front
12 holes x 18 holes
Cut 1

COLOR KEY	
Yards	**Medium Weight Yarn**
32 (29.3m)	■ Lavender
29 (26.6m)	▨ Pink
17 (15.6m)	■ Green
15 (13.8m)	▢ Yellow
14 (12.9m)	▨ Light green
6 (5.5m)	▢ White
5 (4.6m)	■ Rose
4 (3.7m)	▨ Light blue
4 (3.7m)	▨ Gray
1 (1m)	■ Black
1 (1m)	■ Blue
1 (1m)	▨ Dark gold
1 (1m)	▨ Gold
	╱ Black (2-ply) Backstitch

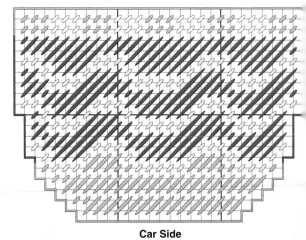

Car Side
28 holes x 20 holes
Cut 8, stitch 4

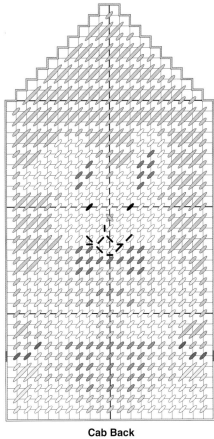

Cab Back
20 holes x 39 holes
Cut 1

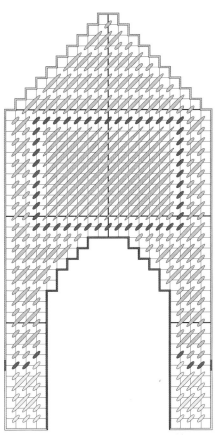

Cab Front
20 holes x 39 holes
Cut 1

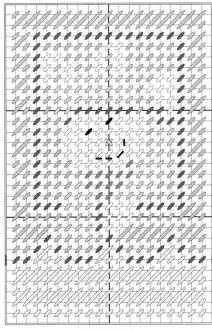

Cab Side A
20 holes x 30 holes
Cut 1

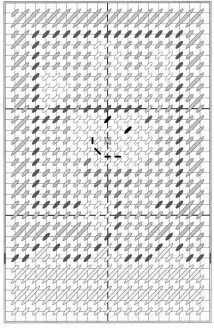

Cab Side B
20 holes x 30 holes
Cut 1

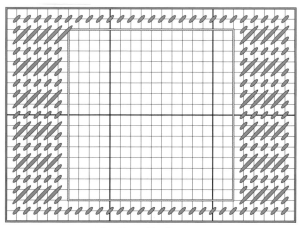

Car Base Top/Bottom
28 holes x 20 holes
Cut 2, stitch 1

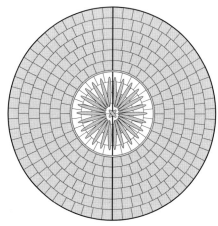

Large Wheel
Cut 4 from 3-inch
radial circles,
cutting away gray areas

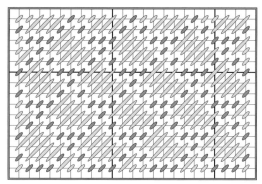

Cab Roof
24 holes x 16 holes
Cut 2

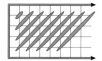

Car Base Side
28 holes x 5 holes
Cut 2

Car Base End
20 holes x 5 holes
Cut 2

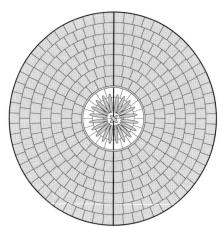

Small Wheel
Cut 8 from 3-inch
radial circles,
cutting away gray areas

COLOR KEY

Yards	Medium Weight Yarn
32 (29.3m)	■ Lavender
29 (26.6m)	■ Pink
17 (15.6m)	■ Green
15 (13.8m)	□ Yellow
14 (12.9m)	■ Light green
6 (5.5m)	□ White
5 (4.6m)	■ Rose
4 (3.7m)	■ Light blue
4 (3.7m)	■ Gray
1 (1m)	■ Black
1 (1m)	■ Blue
1 (1m)	■ Dark gold
1 (1m)	■ Gold
	╱ Black (2-ply) Backstitch

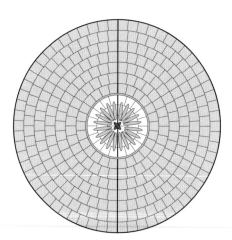

Headlamp
Cut 1 from 3-inch
radial circle,
cutting away gray areas

Fourth of July Express

Size: **Locomotive:** 8¼ inches W x 6⅛ inches H x
3⅝ inches D (21cm x 15.6cm x 9.2cm)
Car: 4½ inches W x 2½ inches H x
3¼ inches D (11.4cm x 6.4cm x 8.3cm)
Skill Level: Beginner

Materials
- ❏ 3 sheets clear 7-count plastic canvas
- ❏ 13 (3-inch) plastic canvas radial circles
- ❏ Medium weight yarn as listed in color key
- ❏ Uniek Needloft metallic craft cord as listed
  in color key
- ❏ 1½ inches (3.8cm) chain
- ❏ 1-inch (2.5cm) gold bell
- ❏ 2 (2-inch/5.1cm) pieces white stem wire
- ❏ #16 tapestry needle
- ❏ Hot-glue gun

Stitching Step by Step
Locomotive

1 Cut engine sides piece, engine front, cab sides A and B, cab front and back, two cab roofs, four bell bracket sides, two bell bracket tops and engine/cab base from 7-count plastic canvas according to graphs. Also cut four strips 1 hole x 12 holes for wheel rods; and one strip 2 holes x 25 holes for headlamp sides.

2 Cut one headlamp and eight wheels from plastic canvas circles according to graphs, cutting away gray areas.

3 Stitch engine sides and front; cab sides, front, back and roofs; headlamp and wheels according to graphs. Stitch bell bracket sides and tops according to graphs, reversing two sides and one top before stitching. Base will remain unstitched.

4 When background stitching is complete, Backstitch engineer's mouth on cab sides using 2 plies separated from a length of red yarn.

5 Using white/gold metallic craft cord throughout, work Continental Stitches down center of headlamp sides strip; Overcast one long edge. Overcast wheel rods and wheels.

6 *Engine:* Gently bend engine sides around engine front, matching red dots. Using dark red and royal blue yarn according to graphs, Whipstitch engine front to engine sides.

7 *Cab:* Using royal blue yarn throughout, Whipstitch cab front, sides and back together along corners, making sure engineers face toward front of locomotive. Overcast top edges. Whipstitch curved back edge of engine sides to cutout edge of cab front.

8 Using dark red and royal blue yarn according to graphs, Whipstitch assembled cab/engine to unstitched base.

9 *Roof:* Using dark red yarn throughout, Whipstitch roof pieces together along one long edge; Overcast remaining edges. Hot-glue roof to cab.

10 *Bell bracket:* Referring to assembly diagram (page 15) and using craft cord throughout, Whipstitch ends of one bell bracket top to inner edges of two bell bracket sides, top edges even; repeat with remaining pieces. Whipstitch bell bracket halves together, wrong sides facing. Hot-glue bell to bracket so that it appears to hang from top.

11 *Headlamp:* Gently bend headlamp sides strip into a ring. Using craft cord throughout, Whipstitch ring to edge of headlamp, Whipstitching ends of ring together. Overcast unfinished edge.

12 *Assembly:* Referring to photo throughout, hot-glue headlamp to engine front; hot-glue bell bracket to engine. Hot-glue two wheels and wheel rod to each side of cab with bottom edges even. Hot-glue two wheels and wheel rod to each side of engine with bottom edges even.

Car

1 Cut four car sides and four car ends from 7-count plastic canvas according to graphs. Also cut two strips 1 hole x 12 holes for wheel rods; and one piece 28 holes x 20 holes for car base.

2 Cut four wheels from plastic canvas circles according to graph, cutting away gray areas.

3 Stitch two car sides, two car ends and all wheels according to graphs. Remaining car sides, ends and base will remain unstitched.

4 Using white/gold metallic craft cord, Overcast wheel rods and wheels.

5 Holding an unstitched piece against the reverse side of a matching car side or end, Whipstitch car sides and ends together along corners using royal blue yarn and working through all layers.

6 Using royal blue yarn throughout, Whipstitch assembled car to base, working through all layers. Whipstitch top edges.

7 *Assembly:* Referring to photo throughout, hot-glue two wheels and wheel rod to each side of car with bottom edges even. Using stem wire, attach ends of chain to car and locomotive.

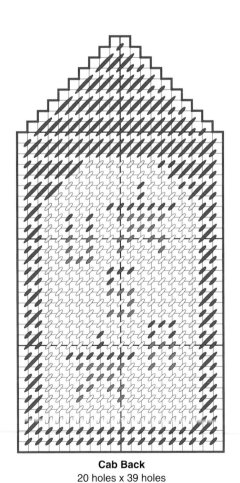

Cab Back
20 holes x 39 holes
Cut 1

Cab Front
20 holes x 39 holes
Cut 1

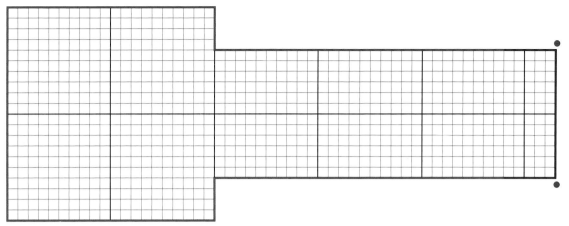

Engine/Cab Base
53 holes x 20 holes
Cut 1, do not stitch

COLOR KEY	
Yards	**Medium Weight Yarn**
40 (36.6m)	■ Royal blue
23 (21.1m)	■ Red
10 (9.2m)	□ White
7 (6.5m)	■ Dark red
3 (2.8m)	▨ Gray
1 (1m)	▨ Medium royal blue
1 (1m)	▨ Peach
	✎ Red (2-ply) Backstitch
	Metallic Craft Cord
17 (15.6m)	□ White/gold #55007

Color number given is for Uniek Needloft metallic craft cord.

Engine Sides
42 holes x 33 holes
Cut 1

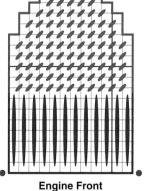

Engine Front
12 holes x 18 holes
Cut 1

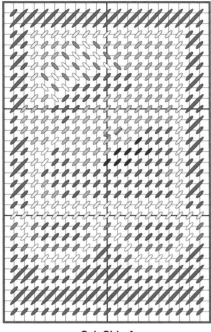

Cab Side A
20 holes x 30 holes
Cut 1

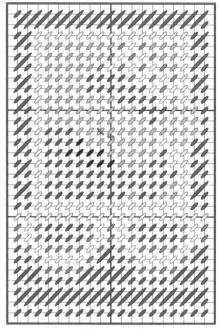

Cab Side B
20 holes x 30 holes
Cut 1

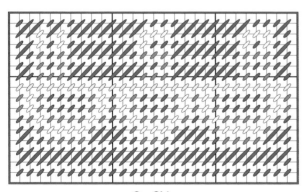

Car Side
28 holes x 16 holes
Cut 4, stitch 2

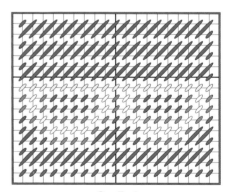

Car End
20 holes x 16 holes
Cut 4, stitch 2

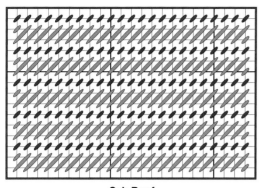

Cab Roof
24 holes x 16 holes
Cut 2

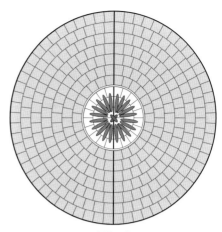

Wheel
Cut 12 from 3-inch
radial circles,
cutting away gray areas

Bell Bracket Side
3 holes x 17 holes
Cut 4, reverse 2

Bell Bracket Top
8 holes x 3 holes
Cut 2, reverse 1

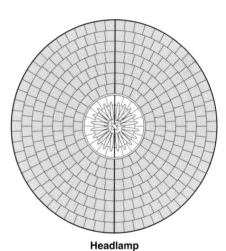

Headlamp
Cut 1 from 3-inch
radial circle,
cutting away gray areas

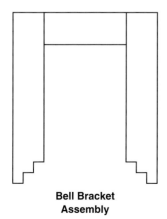

**Bell Bracket
Assembly**

COLOR KEY

Yards	Medium Weight Yarn
40 (36.6m)	■ Royal blue
23 (21.1m)	■ Red
10 (9.2m)	☐ White
7 (6.5m)	■ Dark red
3 (2.8m)	■ Gray
1 (1m)	■ Medium royal blue
1 (1m)	■ Peach
	⁄ Red (2-ply) Backstitch
Metallic Craft Cord	
17 (15.6m)	☐ White/gold #55007

Color number given is for Uniek Needloft
metallic craft cord.

Halloween Express

Size: **Locomotive:** 8¼ inches W x 4⅝ inches H x
3¾ inches D (21cm x 11.8cm x 9.5cm)
Car: 4¼ inches W x 3 inches H x
3⅜ inches D (12.4cm x 7.6cm x 8.6cm)
Skill Level: Beginner

Materials

❏ 3 sheets clear 7-count plastic canvas
❏ 13 (3-inch) plastic canvas radial circles
❏ Medium weight yarn as listed in color key
❏ 1½ inches (3.8cm) chain
❏ 2 (2-inch/5.1cm) pieces white stem wire
❏ #16 tapestry needle
❏ Hot-glue gun

Stitching Step by Step

Locomotive

1 Cut engine sides piece, engine front, cab sides A
and B, cab front and back, cab roof, two smokestack
sides, smokestack front/back piece and engine/cab base
from 7-count plastic canvas according to graphs. Also cut
four strips 1 hole x 12 holes for wheel rods; and one strip
2 holes x 25 holes for headlamp sides.

2 Cut one headlamp, four small wheels and four large
wheels from plastic canvas circles according to
graphs, cutting away gray areas.

3 Stitch engine sides and front; cab sides, front,
back and roof; smokestack sides and front/back;
headlamp and wheels according to graphs. Base will
remain unstitched.

4 When background stitching is complete, Backstitch
ghost's mouth on cab sides and back, and jack-o'-
lantern faces on smokestack sides using 2 plies separated
from a length of black yarn.

5 Using green yarn, work Continental Stitches down
center of headlamp sides strip; Overcast one long
edge. Using medium brown yarn, Overcast all wheel rods.
Using orange yarn, Overcast all wheels.

6 *Engine:* Gently bend engine sides around engine
front, matching red dots. Using dark brown yarn,
Whipstitch engine front to engine sides.

7 *Cab:* Using orange yarn throughout, Whipstitch
cab front, sides and back together along side
edges, making sure ghost engineers face toward front of
locomotive. Whipstitch roof to assembled cab.

8 Using dark brown yarn, Whipstitch curved back edge of engine sides to cutout edge of cab front. Using orange and dark brown yarn according to graphs, Whipstitch assembled cab/engine to unstitched base.

9 *Smokestack:* Gently bend smokestack front/back piece around edge of one smokestack side piece, matching red dots at bottom of smokestack. Using orange yarn throughout, Whipstitch side to front/back piece. Whipstitch remaining side piece to unfinished edge; Overcast bottom edges.

10 *Headlamp:* Gently bend headlamp sides strip into a ring. Using green yarn throughout, Whipstitch ring to edge of headlamp, Whipstitching ends of ring together. Overcast unfinished edge.

11 *Assembly:* Referring to photo throughout, hot-glue headlamp to engine front; hot-glue smokestack to engine. Hot-glue two large wheels and wheel rod to each side of cab with bottom edges even. Hot-glue two small wheels and wheel rod to each side of engine with bottom edges even.

Car

1 Cut four car sides, four car ends, two car base top/bottom pieces, two car base sides and two car base ends from 7-count plastic canvas according to graphs. Also cut two strips 1 hole x 12 holes for wheel rods.

2 Cut four small wheels from plastic canvas circles according to graph, cutting away gray areas.

3 Stitch two car sides, two car ends, one car base top/bottom piece, both car base sides, both car base ends and all wheels according to graphs. Remaining car sides, car ends and second base top/bottom piece will remain unstitched.

4 Using medium brown yarn, Overcast wheel rods. Using orange yarn, Overcast wheels.

5 Holding an unstitched piece against the reverse side of a matching car side or end, and using orange yarn through step 6, Whipstitch car sides and ends together along corners, working through all layers.

6 Whipstitch bottom edges of assembled car sides and ends to stitched base top, around edges of unstitched area in center. Whipstitch top edges of car sides and ends.

7 *Base:* Using green yarn throughout, Whipstitch ends of car base side and end strips together to form shallow rectangle. Whipstitch assembled sides and ends to unstitched car base bottom. Whipstitch remaining edges to car base top.

8 *Assembly:* Referring to photo throughout, hot-glue two wheels and wheel rod to each side of car with bottom edges even. Using stem wire, attach ends of chain to car and locomotive.

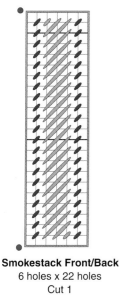

Smokestack Front/Back
6 holes x 22 holes
Cut 1

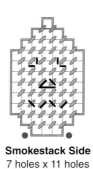

Smokestack Side
7 holes x 11 holes
Cut 2

COLOR KEY	
Yards	**Medium Weight Yarn**
46 (42.1m)	▨ Orange
21 (19.3m)	■ Rust
13 (11.9m)	▨ Green
13 (11.9m)	▨ Medium brown
13 (11.9m)	■ Dark brown
6 (5.5m)	□ Light orange
5 (4.6m)	□ White
2 (1.9m)	□ Yellow
1 (1m)	■ Black
	╱ Black (2-ply) Backstitch

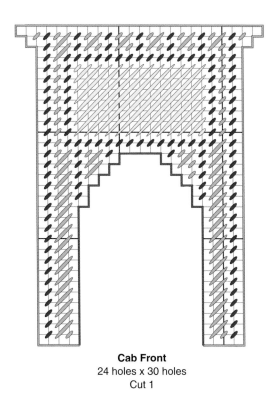

Cab Front
24 holes x 30 holes
Cut 1

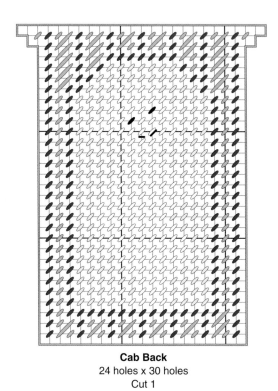

Cab Back
24 holes x 30 holes
Cut 1

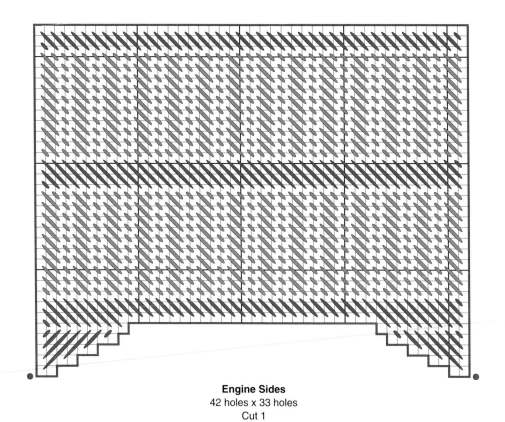

Engine Sides
42 holes x 33 holes
Cut 1

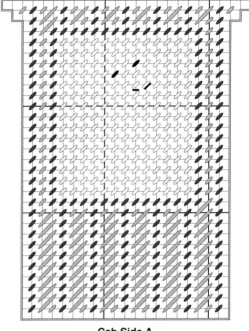

Cab Side A
24 holes x 30 holes
Cut 1

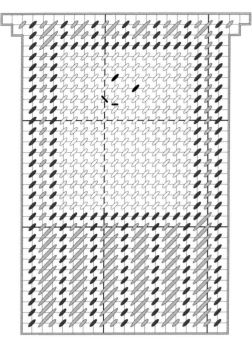

Cab Side B
24 holes x 30 holes
Cut 1

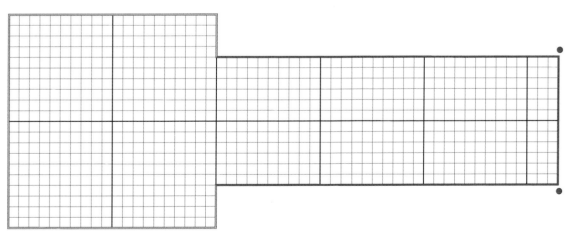

Engine/Cab Base
53 holes x 20 holes
Cut 1, do not stitch

COLOR KEY	
Yards	**Medium Weight Yarn**
46 (42.1m)	Orange
21 (19.3m)	Rust
13 (11.9m)	Green
13 (11.9m)	Medium brown
13 (11.9m)	Dark brown
6 (5.5m)	Light orange
5 (4.6m)	White
2 (1.9m)	Yellow
1 (1m)	Black
✄	Black (2-ply) Backstitch

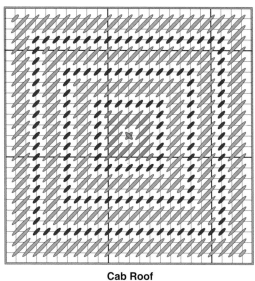

Cab Roof
24 holes x 24 holes
Cut 1

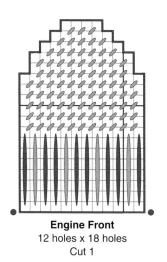

Engine Front
12 holes x 18 holes
Cut 1

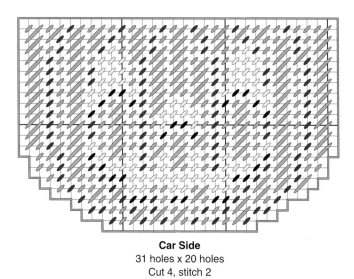

Car Side
31 holes x 20 holes
Cut 4, stitch 2

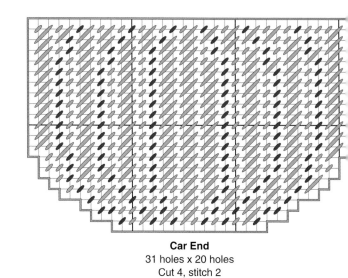

Car End
31 holes x 20 holes
Cut 4, stitch 2

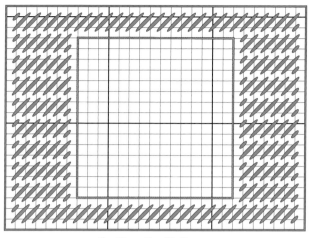

Car Base Top/Bottom
29 holes x 21 holes
Cut 2, stitch 1

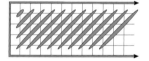

Car Base Side
29 holes x 5 holes
Cut 2

Car Base End
21 holes x 5 holes
Cut 2

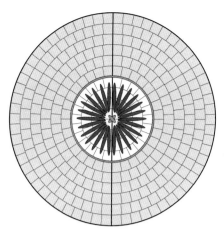

Large Wheel
Cut 4 from 3-inch
radial circles,
cutting away gray areas

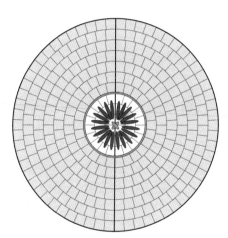

Small Wheel
Cut 8 from 3-inch
radial circles,
cutting away gray areas

COLOR KEY

Yards	Medium Weight Yarn
46 (42.1m)	▨ Orange
21 (19.3m)	■ Rust
13 (11.9m)	▨ Green
13 (11.9m)	▨ Medium brown
13 (11.9m)	■ Dark brown
6 (5.5m)	☐ Light orange
5 (4.6m)	☐ White
2 (1.9m)	☐ Yellow
1 (1m)	■ Black
	╱ Black (2-ply) Backstitch

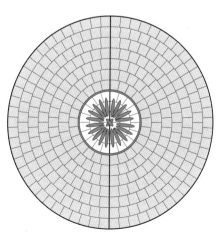

Headlamp
Cut 1 from 3-inch
radial circle,
cutting away gray areas

Thanksgiving Express

Size: **Locomotive:** 8 inches W x 6⅛ inches H x
3½ inches D (20.3cm x 15.6cm x 8.9cm)
Car: 4⅜ inches W x 2⅞ inches H x
3⅜ inches D (11.2cm x 7.3cm x 8.6cm)
Skill Level: Beginner

Materials

- ❏ 3 sheets clear 7-count plastic canvas
- ❏ 14 (3-inch) plastic canvas radial circles
- ❏ Medium weight yarn as listed in color key
- ❏ 1½ inches (3.8cm) chain
- ❏ 2 (2-inch/5.1cm) pieces white stem wire
- ❏ #16 tapestry needle
- ❏ Hot-glue gun

Stitching Step by Step

Locomotive

1 Cut engine sides piece, engine front, cab sides A and
B, cab front and back, two cab roofs, smokestack
and smokestack ring, and engine/cab base from 7-count
plastic canvas according to graphs. Also cut four strips 1
hole x 12 holes for wheel rods; and one strip 2 holes x 25
holes for headlamp sides.

2 Cut one headlamp, one smokestack top, four sma[ll]
wheels and four large wheels from plastic canva[s]
circles according to graphs, cutting away gray areas.

3 Stitch engine sides and front; cab sides, fron[t,]
back and roofs; smokestack, smokestack ring an[d]
smokestack top; headlamp and wheels according to graph[s.]
Base will remain unstitched.

4 When background stitching is complete, Backstitc[h]
pilgrims' mouths on cab sides and back usin[g]
2 plies separated from a length of red yarn.

5 Using green yarn, work Continental Stitches dow[n]
center of headlamp sides strip; Overcast one lon[g]
edge. Using medium brown yarn, Overcast all wheel rod[s.]
Using light brown yarn, Overcast all wheels.

6 *Engine:* Gently bend engine sides around engin[e]
front, matching red dots. Using light brown an[d]
dark brown yarn, Whipstitch engine front to engine side[s]
according to graphs.

7 *Cab:* Using light brown yarn throughout, Whipstit[ch]
cab front, sides and back together along side edge[s,]
making sure pilgrim engineers face toward front [of]
locomotive. Overcast top edges. Whipstitch curved ba[ck]
edge of engine sides to cutout edge of cab front.

8 Using light brown and dark brown yarn according to graphs, Whipstitch assembled cab/engine to unstitched base.

9 *Roof:* Using medium brown yarn throughout, Whipstitch roof pieces together along one long edge; overcast remaining edges. Hot-glue roof to cab.

10 *Smokestack:* Gently bend smokestack ring strip into a ring. Using medium brown yarn throughout, Whipstitch ends together. Whipstitch ring to edge of smokestack top. Gently bend smokestack into a ring; Whipstitch short ends to form column. Whipstitch assembled ring/top to top of smokestack column; Overcast bottom edge.

11 *Headlamp:* Gently bend headlamp sides strip into a ring. Using green yarn throughout, Whipstitch ring to edge of headlamp, Whipstitching ends of ring together. Overcast unfinished edge.

12 *Assembly:* Referring to photo throughout, hot-glue headlamp to engine front; hot-glue smokestack to engine. Hot-glue two large wheels and wheel rod to each side of cab with bottom edges even. Hot-glue two small wheels and wheel rod to each side of engine with bottom edges even.

Car

1 Cut four car sides and four car ends from 7-count plastic canvas according to graph. Also cut two strips 1 hole x 12 holes for wheel rods; and one piece 28 holes x 20 holes for car base.

2 Cut four small wheels from plastic canvas circles according to graph, cutting away gray areas.

3 Stitch two car sides, two car ends and all wheels according to graphs. Remaining car sides, ends and base will remain unstitched.

4 Using medium brown yarn, Overcast wheel rods. Using light brown yarn, Overcast wheels.

5 Holding an unstitched piece against the reverse side of a matching car side or end, Whipstitch car sides and ends together along corners using medium brown yarn and working through all layers.

6 Using medium brown yarn throughout, Whipstitch assembled car to base, working through all layers. Whipstitch top edges.

7 *Assembly:* Referring to photo throughout, hot-glue two wheels and wheel rod to each side of car with bottom edges even. Using stem wire, attach ends of chain to car and locomotive.

COLOR KEY

Yards	Medium Weight Yarn
41 (37.5m)	□ Light brown
35 (32.1m)	▤ Medium brown
10 (9.2m)	▢ Beige
8 (7.4m)	▧ Dark brown
3 (2.8m)	□ White
3 (2.8m)	▨ Dusty blue
2 (1.9m)	■ Black
2 (1.9m)	▥ Green
2 (1.9m)	▢ Peach
(1m)	▤ Dark dusty blue
(1m)	▨ Gray
(1m)	╱ Red (2-ply) Backstitch

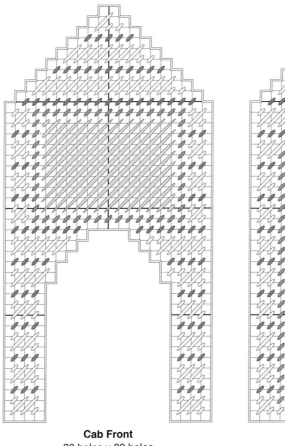

Cab Front
20 holes x 39 holes
Cut 1

Cab Back
20 holes x 39 holes
Cut 1

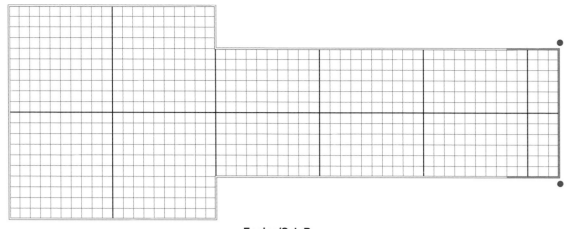

Engine/Cab Base
53 holes x 20 holes
Cut 1, do not stitch

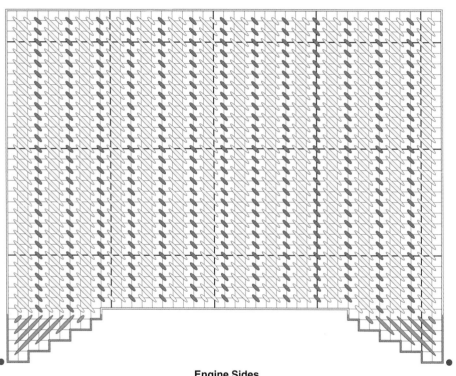

Engine Sides
42 holes x 33 holes
Cut 1

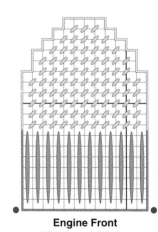

Engine Front
12 holes x 18 holes
Cut 1

COLOR KEY

Yards	Medium Weight Yarn
41 (37.5m)	☐ Light brown
35 (32.1m)	■ Medium brown
10 (9.2m)	☐ Beige
8 (7.4m)	■ Dark brown
3 (2.8m)	☐ White
3 (2.8m)	☐ Dusty blue
2 (1.9m)	■ Black
2 (1.9m)	■ Green
2 (1.9m)	☐ Peach
1 (1m)	■ Dark dusty blue
1 (1m)	☐ Gray
1 (1m)	✒ Red (2-ply) Backstitch

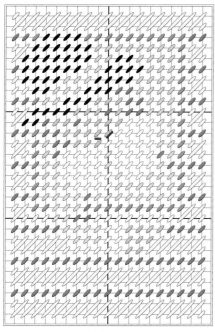

Cab Side A
20 holes x 30 holes
Cut 1

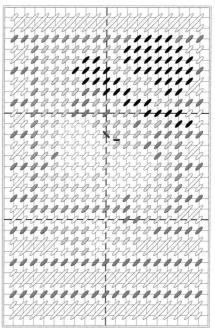

Cab Side B
20 holes x 30 holes
Cut 1

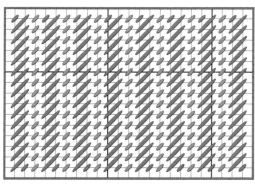

Cab Roof
24 holes x 16 holes
Cut 2

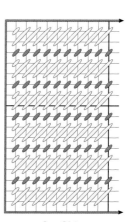

Car Side
28 holes x 18 holes
Cut 4, stitch 2

Car End
20 holes x 18 holes
Cut 4, stitch 2

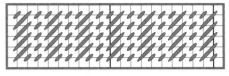

Smokestack
21 holes x 6 holes
Cut 1

Smokestack Ring
24 holes x 3 holes
Cut 1

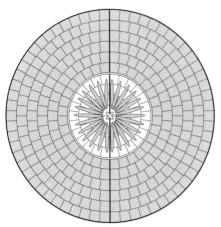

Large Wheel
Cut 4 from 3-inch
radial circles,
cutting away gray areas

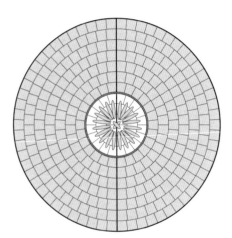

Smokestack Top
Cut 1 from 3-inch
radial circle,
cutting away gray areas

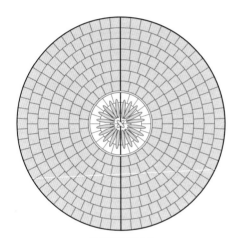

Small Wheel
Cut 8 from 3-inch
radial circles,
cutting away gray areas

COLOR KEY	
Yards	**Medium Weight Yarn**
41 (37.5m)	☐ Light brown
35 (32.1m)	▨ Medium brown
10 (9.2m)	☐ Beige
8 (7.4m)	▨ Dark brown
3 (2.8m)	☐ White
3 (2.8m)	▨ Dusty blue
2 (1.9m)	■ Black
2 (1.9m)	▨ Green
2 (1.9m)	☐ Peach
1 (1m)	▨ Dark dusty blue
1 (1m)	▨ Gray
1 (1m)	✏ Red (2-ply) Backstitch

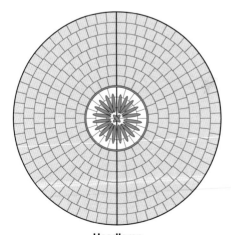

Headlamp
Cut 1 from 3-inch
radial circle,
cutting away gray areas

Santa's Express

Size: **Locomotive:** 8¼ inches W x 4⅝ inches H x
3¾ inches D (21cm x 11.8cm x 9.5cm)
Car: 4¼ inches W x 3 inches H x
3⅜ inches D (12.4cm x 7.6cm x 8.6cm)
Skill Level: Beginner

Materials
❑ 3 sheets clear 7-count plastic canvas
❑ 13 (3-inch) plastic canvas radial circles
❑ Medium weight yarn as listed in color key
❑ Uniek Needloft metallic craft cord as listed
   in color key
❑ 1½ inches (3.8cm) chain
❑ 2 (2-inch/5.1cm) pieces white stem wire
❑ #16 tapestry needle
❑ Hot-glue gun

Stitching Step by Step

Locomotive

1 Cut engine sides piece, engine front, cab sides A
and B, cab front and back, cab roof, two smokestack
sides, smokestack front/back piece and engine/cab base
from 7-count plastic canvas according to graphs. Also cut
four strips 1 hole x 12 holes for wheel rods; and one strip
holes x 25 holes for headlamp sides.

2 Cut one headlamp, four small wheels and four large
wheels from plastic canvas circles according to
graphs, cutting away gray areas.

3 Stitch engine sides and front; cab sides, front,
back and roof; smokestack sides and front/back;
headlamp and wheels according to graphs. Base will
remain unstitched.

4 When background stitching is complete, Backstitch
Santa's mustache on cab sides using 2 plies
separated from a length of gray yarn; Backstitch Mrs.
Santa's mouth on cab back using 2 plies separated from a
length of red yarn.

5 Using white/gold metallic craft cord throughout,
work Continental Stitches down center of headlamp
sides strip; Overcast one long edge. Overcast all wheel
rods. Using red and white yarn throughout, Overcast all
wheels according to graphs.

6 *Engine:* Gently bend engine sides around engine
front, matching red dots. Using craft cord and dark
red yarn according to graphs, Whipstitch engine front to
engine sides.

7 *Cab:* Using dark red yarn, Whipstitch cab front,
sides and back together along side edges, making
sure Santa engineers face toward front of locomotive.

8 Using dark red yarn, Whipstitch roof to assembled cab; Whipstitch curved back edge of engine sides to cutout edge of cab front. Using dark red yarn and craft cord according to graphs, Whipstitch assembled cab/engine to unstitched base.

9 *Smokestack:* Gently bend smokestack front/back piece around edge of one smokestack side piece, matching red dots at bottom of smokestack. Using red yarn throughout, Whipstitch side to front/back piece. Whipstitch remaining side piece to unfinished edge; Overcast bottom edges.

10 *Headlamp:* Gently bend headlamp sides strip into a ring. Using craft cord throughout, Whipstitch ring to edge of headlamp, Whipstitching ends of ring together. Overcast unfinished edge.

11 *Assembly:* Referring to photo throughout, hot-glue headlamp to engine front; hot-glue smokestack to engine. Hot-glue two large wheels and wheel rod to each side of cab with bottom edges even. Hot-glue two small wheels and wheel rod to each side of engine with bottom edges even.

Car

1 Cut four car sides and four car ends from 7-count plastic canvas according to graphs. Also cut two strips 1 hole x 12 holes for wheel rods; and one piece 28 holes x 21 holes for car base.

2 Cut four small wheels from plastic canvas circles according to graph, cutting away gray areas.

3 Stitch two car sides, two car ends and all wheels according to graphs. Remaining car sides, ends and base will remain unstitched.

4 When background stitching is complete, Backstitch bows on wreaths on car sides using white/gold metallic craft cord.

5 Using craft cord, Overcast wheel rods. Using red and white yarns, Overcast wheels according to graph.

6 Holding an unstitched piece against the reverse side of a matching car side or end, Whipstitch car sides and ends together along corners using dark red yarn and working through all layers.

7 Using dark red yarn throughout, Whipstitch assembled car to base, working through all layers. Whipstitch top edges.

8 *Assembly:* Referring to photo throughout, hot-glue two wheels and wheel rod to each side of car with bottom edges even. Using stem wire, attach ends of chain to car and locomotive.

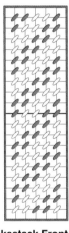

Smokestack Front/Back
6 holes x 20 holes
Cut 1

Smokestack Side
8 holes x 9 holes
Cut 2

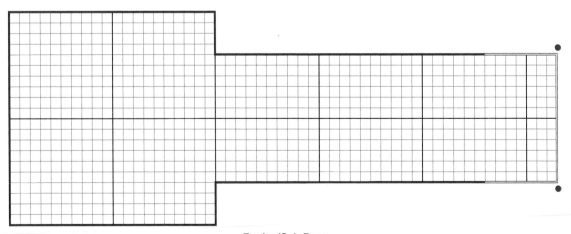

Engine/Cab Base
53 holes x 20 holes
Cut 1, do not stitch

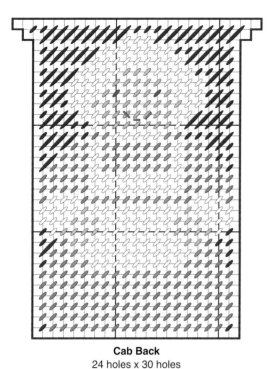

Cab Back
24 holes x 30 holes
Cut 1

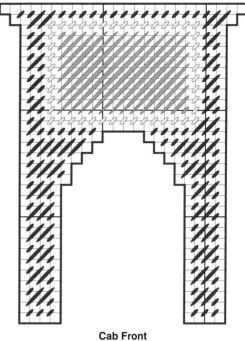

Cab Front
24 holes x 30 holes
Cut 1

COLOR KEY	
Yards	**Medium Weight Yarn**
43 (39.4m)	■ Dark red
18 (16.5m)	■ Red
15 (13.8m)	□ White
5 (4.6m)	■ Green
4 (3.7m)	▨ Light green
3 (2.8m)	■ Gray
2 (1.9m)	▨ Peach
1 (1m)	■ Blue
	✎ Red (2-ply) Backstitch
	✎ Gray (2-ply) Backstitch
	Metallic Craft Cord
17 (15.6m)	□ White/gold #55007
	✎ White/gold #55007 Backstitch

Color number given is for Uniek Needloft metallic craft cord.

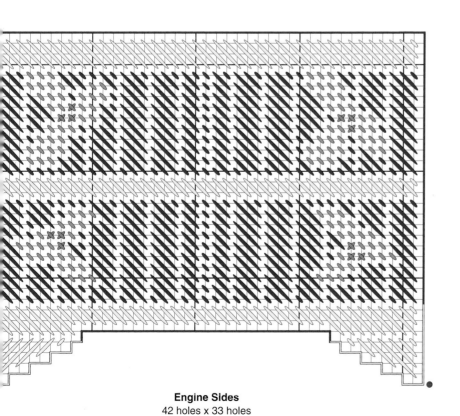

Engine Sides
42 holes x 33 holes
Cut 1

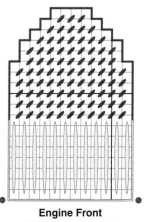

Engine Front
12 holes x 18 holes
Cut 1

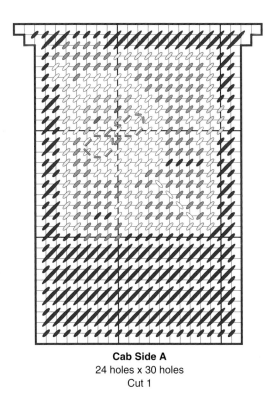

Cab Side A
24 holes x 30 holes
Cut 1

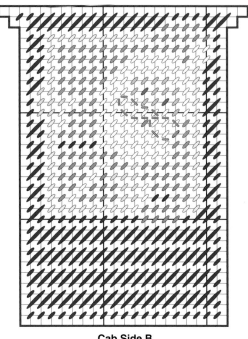

Cab Side B
24 holes x 30 holes
Cut 1

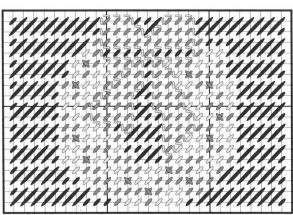

Car Side
28 holes x 19 holes
Cut 4, stitch 2

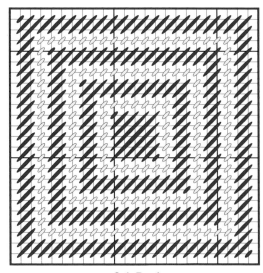

Cab Roof
24 holes x 24 holes
Cut 1

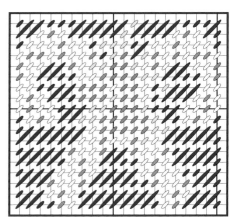

Car End
21 holes x 19 holes
Cut 4, stitch 2

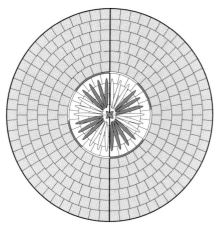

Large Wheel
Cut 4 from 3-inch
radial circles,
cutting away gray areas

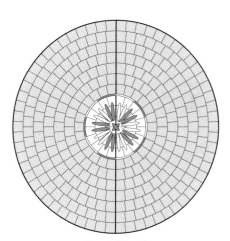

Small Wheel
Cut 8 from 3-inch
radial circles,
cutting away gray areas

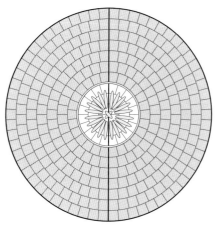

Headlamp
Cut 1 from 3-inch
radial circle,
cutting away gray areas

COLOR KEY

Yards	Medium Weight Yarn
43 (39.4m)	■ Dark red
18 (16.5m)	■ Red
15 (13.8m)	□ White
5 (4.6m)	■ Green
4 (3.7m)	▨ Light green
3 (2.8m)	■ Gray
2 (1.9m)	▨ Peach
1 (1m)	■ Blue
	╱ Red (2-ply) Backstitch
	╱ Gray (2-ply) Backstitch
	Metallic Craft Cord
17 (15.6m)	□ White/gold #55007
	╱ White/gold #55007 Backstitch

Color number given is for Uniek Needloft metallic craft cord.

The full line of The Needlecraft Shop
products is carried by Annie's Attic catalog.
TOLL-FREE ORDER LINE
or to request a free catalog
(800) 582-6643
Customer Service
(800) 449-0440
Visit AnniesAttic.com

We have made every effort to ensure the accuracy
and completeness of these instructions. We cannot,
however, be responsible for human error, typographical
mistakes or variations in individual work.

ISBN: 978-1-57367-339-6

Printed in USA

2 3 4 5 6 7 8 9

Getting Started

Before You Cut

Buy one brand of canvas for each entire project as brands can dif-
fer slightly in the distance between bars. Count holes carefully from
graph before you cut, using the bolder lines that show each 10 hole.
These 10-count lines begin in the lower left corner of each graph to
make counting easier. Mark canvas before cutting; then remove all marks
completely before stitching. If the piece is cut in a rectangular or square
shape and is either not worked, or worked with only one color and
one type of stitch, the graph is not included in the pattern. Instead, the
cutting and stitching instructions are given in the general instructions
with the individual project instructions.

Covering the Canvas

Bring needle up from back of work, leaving a short length of yarn at
back of canvas; work over short length to secure. To end a thread, weave
needle and thread through the wrong side of your last few stitches; cut.
Follow the numbers on the small graphs beside each stitch illustration; bring
your needle up from the back of the work on odd numbers and down through
the front of the work on even numbers. Work embroidery stitches last, after
the canvas has been completely covered by the needlepoint stitches.

Shopping for Supplies

For supplies, first shop your local craft
and needlework stores. Some supplies
may be found in fabric, hardware and
discount stores. If you are unable to find
the supplies you need, please call Annie's
Attic at (800) 582-6643 to request a free
catalog that sells plastic canvas supplies.

Basic Stitches

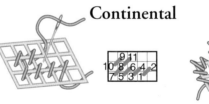

Continental   Overcast   Whipstitch

Slanted
Gobelin   Long   Cross

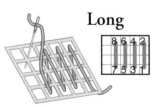

Embroidery Stitches

French Knot   Lazy Daisy   Backstitch   Straight

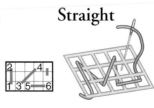

METRIC KEY:
millimeters = (mm)
centimeters = (cm)
meters = (m)
grams = (g)